HOW TO DEAL WITH DIFFICULT PEOPLE

How to Recognize, Analyze, Approach, and Deal With Difficult People

(Learn How to Communicate Effectively With Difficult People)

James Miller

Published by Sharon Lohan

© **James Miller**

All Rights Reserved

How to Deal With Difficult People: How to Recognize, Analyze, Approach, and Deal With Difficult People (Learn How to Communicate Effectively With Difficult People)

ISBN 978-1-990334-72-6

All rights reserved. No part of this guide may be reproduced in any form without permission in writing from the publisher except in the case of brief quotations embodied in critical articles or reviews.

Legal & Disclaimer

The information contained in this book is not designed to replace or take the place of any form of medicine or professional medical advice. The information in this book has been provided for educational and entertainment purposes only.

The information contained in this book has been compiled from sources deemed reliable, and it is accurate to the best of the Author's knowledge; however, the Author cannot guarantee its accuracy and validity and cannot be held liable for any errors or omissions. Changes are periodically made to this book. You must consult your doctor or get professional medical advice before using any of the suggested remedies, techniques, or information in this book.

Upon using the information contained in this book, you agree to hold harmless the Author from and against any damages, costs, and expenses, including any legal fees potentially resulting from the application of any of the information provided by this guide. This disclaimer applies to any damages or injury caused by the use and application, whether directly or indirectly, of any advice or information presented, whether for breach of contract, tort, negligence, personal injury, criminal intent, or under any other cause of action.

You agree to accept all risks of using the information presented inside this book. You need to consult a professional medical practitioner in order to ensure you are both able and healthy enough to participate in this program.

Table of Contents

INTRODUCTION 1

CHAPTER 1: DIFFICULT PEOPLE 101: TYPES AND CHARACTERISTICS 3

CHAPTER 2: HOW TO DEAL WITH DIFFICULT PEOPLE AT WORK 11

CHAPTER 3: HOW TO MENTOR YOUR TEAM 16

CHAPTER 4: RESOLVING CONFLICTS 30

CHAPTER 5: DISRESPECTFUL EMPLOYEES 57

CHAPTER 6: FIND A COMMON THREAD AND SEW IT UP!. 67

CHAPTER 7: THE POWER OF WORDS IN DEALING WITH A DIFFICULT PERSON 70

CHAPTER 8: PRACTICAL EXAMPLES ON HOW TO DEAL WITH DIFFICULT PEOPLE.. 79

CHAPTER 9: HOW TO HANDLE DIFFICULT TOPICS 118

CHAPTER 10: HOW TO DEAL WITH A TACTLESS PERSON 125

CHAPTER 11: REFLECT DIFFICULT BEHAVIOR BACK 129

CHAPTER 12: DON'T BE AFRAID TO SET CONSEQUENCES 137

CHAPTER 13: HOW TO DEAL WITH A DIFFICULT FAMILY MEMBER 141

CHAPTER 14: IDENTIFYING AND MANAGING YOUR DIFFICULT PERSONALITY TRAITS IN CONFLICT 145

CONCLUSION 150

Introduction

As the day goes by, everyone has to meet a frustrating situation along the line. Sometimes we just feel like people are not good enough for us. Sometimes we may be angry at the world and begin to ask for reasons things are not going the way we want.

Rejection also becomes a source of frustration in the common world. You don't need to be utterly or verbally rejected in order to feel the frustration.

Another side of frustration is disappointment. This is the most common cause of frustration and you have to be mentally strong in order to be able to deal with both on a daily basis.

Sometimes being able to deal with frustration means taking the step towards making yourself the hero, the star, instead of always being the victim. Most people resort to self-defeating reactions which only push them under the wheels and they stay victimized as long as the adversary needs them to be.

This book is dedicated to you who want to transform frustration with happiness, patience and breakthrough.

Chapter 1: Difficult People 101: Types And Characteristics

As indicated in the introduction, difficult people are a part of your daily life and crossing paths with them is something you cannot avoid. You should know that things do not just happen. There is a reason to every action. As such, to deal with difficult people, you must become proactive. The first step towards effectively dealing with difficult people is to define the nature of their difficult problem. Then try to understand where they are coming from.

Can it be that something awful recently happened in that person's life and that is perhaps why he or she is being difficult?

Does that person simply want to intimidate you?

Is being difficult a cultural tendency?

Is being difficult part of that person's personality style?

To make it easier to identify some common difficult personalities and their behavior styles, let us highlight the different types of difficult people; this will help you answer some of the above questions.

Types of Difficult People

There are several types of difficult people:

A Maybe Person

A maybe friend or colleague is someone who has trouble making up his or her mind. He or she usually avoids making decisions because of the fear of disappointing you. A good example of this is an instance where you go to watch a movie with two friends and get into an argument on who died first in the movie. If you decide to take a majority wins vote and your maybe friend is the tiebreaker, he or she will avoid taking a vote simply because the residual actions will hurt one of you.

The other characteristic of a maybe friend is that he or she usually procrastinates with the hope of getting a better option. This behavior can be difficult because the results may affect you directly. A good example of this is an instance where you and your fiancée are planning your wedding and you interview a couple of wedding planners. Then you shortlist them and settle on the two names you think are perfect to choose from; you then allow your fiancée to choose which of the two to use. Being a maybe person, your fiancée can procrastinate and delay the decision until you to miss-out on the two planners when they get booked.

Super Agreeable

The other common type of difficult people is the super agreeable type. These types of people tend to agree with everything you say. They are always supportive of your ideas until you require some action from them. Then they go ahead and disappoint you. A good example is planning to be weight loss friends with a friend; if the friend is the super agreeable type, he, or she will agree to hit the gym with you and may even help you look for a good gym; however, when it comes to committing to exercise, your friend deserts you.

This type of people need to agree with everything, pretend to like and care about everyone and give false promises they cannot keep.

Complainers

These types of people are difficult because they will find fault in everything you do because they see the world as a hostile and unfair place. When dealing with this type of person, you will always get complaints. It is sometimes very hard to recognize them because they hide their complaints in real issues. This in turn turns you into a defensive person whenever you are around that person because of the constant blame the person lays on you.

A common trait among complainers is their alleged powerless in dealing with their subject of complaint. Their main aim is usually to complain but shy away from solutions.

The Aggressive Type

These types of difficult people are mostly bullies who intimidate and abuse you. They normally believe you are a weak victim and deserve the kind of treatment they are giving you. These types of people are mostly motivated when you show signs of weakness. They can be categorized into two:

1. There are those who attack you personally by pointing and confronting you angrily even when you are talking about a completely different thing like a project or an idea.

2. Then there are those who feel strongly about how you are supposed to think and act. They think how they act and think is how you should think and act. They normally have rude comments and biting sarcasm.

The Know-It-All

The know it all type of person falls into two categories.

1. The experts: the expert is well informed and productive. These people are mostly full of "themselves" and usually act superior. They also use their knowledge to make you feel stupid. They are impatient with other people's ideas, which they deem inferior, and will never ask for your help.

2. The partially informed: This type of person will argue with you because he or she has a little knowledge about a certain topic. This type of difficult person is difficult to work with because they ignore other people's ideas and opinions.

The Pessimist

Pessimists are the type of people who do not think anything can work. If you seek advice from them, they will discourage and kill your hopes. This type of person never has a solution; he or she only shuts down other people's ideas. They drag you down to a pool of doubts and disappointments. A good example is how you can go to one of your friends and explain your new business idea only for the friend to tell you the business will not work because one of his or her relatives tried that business and miserably failed.

Now that you now have a clearer understanding of the various types of difficult people, let us now look at how to deal with difficult people starting with how to approach them.

Chapter 2: How To Deal With Difficult People At Work

At work, we endeavor to maintain a good working relationship with our co-workers to keep the environment conducive for work. Our outputs reflect the relationship we have with the people we work with, especially if our work is team-based.

Try to be in their shoes

Each person is his own bundle of responsibilities, stressors and problems. Even though we try to keep our personal life separate from our work, these naturally become part of our personality.

So try to step into the shoes of your co-worker. Understanding their situation and position will help you understand their actions. She might be a single mother of a child with special needs. He might be the bread winner as the eldest son, who has to rally funds to support his sick father. This will stretch your patience and renew respect for who they are.

Seek opinion of others

Discuss the situation with others in your workplace. Choose two to three people that you trust to be fair and impartial. If possible, consult with those who have known the person for a long time; talk with the veterans in your office.

Verify that others have the same observations as you do. There is always the possibility that you're the only person who thinks that way. If so, ask suggestions from others on how you can overcome this feeling against your co-worker.

However, if they have the same observations as you do, consult with them on how best to handle the situation.

Talk to them in private

Some people are not aware of their faults or that we are having difficulty working with them. It would be doing them a great favor by letting them know what others have observed and feel about them. Rather than talking about him with your other co-workers, it would be more helpful to talk to the person concerned to address the problem.

Find good timing when you're both calm and not busy and pull him aside for a private conversation. Properly lay down the situation so that he understands that this is not a personal attack. Express your intent to help him.

Maintain a "work only" relationship

The rule of thumb is professionalism. If you do not achieve familiar terms with them, it is perfectly acceptable. Don't break your neck forcing friendship on each other. Remember that at the end of the day, these are people you work with. The most important thing in your relationship is the ability to do the job well and meet the deadlines.

Keep your encounters cool and professional. Do not let any personal judgment get in the way of work and don't take things personally.

Chapter 3: How To Mentor Your Team

You're going to need to make a lot of decisions when you join the big or middle leagues of management; indeed, it's no great stretch to say that it can often be overwhelming. Perhaps one of the very first things you're going to want to decide is the not-so-insignificant matter of what type of boss you want to be.

Do you see yourself issuing orders for others to follow, secure in the knowledge that if they do things your way, it's going to get done? Or perhaps you see yourself more in a paternal or maternal role, guiding your junior employees so that they reap the benefit of your experience. You could even be the sort of manager that prefers listening, offering suggestions and then letting your subordinates make the decisions.

Let me give you my take on this based on my personal experience and hopefully save you a little time while you ponder this question: if you can, try like Hell to avoid the former. Authoritarian bosses (do as I say – now!) may get results but are universally loathed. There's no other way to put it. So, you'd be much better off adopting a democratic and mentoring approach if you want a happy and productive workforce.

What is mentoring? Good question. There are probably as many definitions as there are managers but needless to say mentoring is usually semi-structured guidance by another with the aim of helping an employee to manage their own learning, develop their skills and reach their full potential.

The Oxford English Dictionary describes a mentor as "an experienced and trusted adviser." A mentor is usually older or more experienced and can advise the younger employee on various topics, based on their own knowledge and experience. They may show them how to improve an element of their job performance, advise them on customer service, recommend a particular product or talk to them about their fears and concerns in the workplace. There is no limit to what a good mentor can do.

Some people are natural mentors; they guide and coach their staff without ever feeling the need to put an official title on it or call themselves a 'mentor'. For others, novice and experienced managers alike, mentoring doesn't come easily.

"I was shocked when on the first day of starting my new role, my boss came right out and told me that I wasn't there to mentor staff; I was just there to tell them what to do," says Julie, a middle manager at a retail store. "Needless to say my biggest problem in that job was managing upwards and trying to avoid becoming the same sort of manager as he was!"

Mentoring staff is often overlooked and all too easy to forget when you're trying to cope with the everyday demands of running a team or department. If you're too busy fire-fighting tasks and actions on a daily basis (don't forget to re-read the delegation section!), it's easy to think of mentoring as a luxury that you just can't afford right now.

That said mentoring can be one of the most rewarding aspects of management. It can be hugely beneficial and gratifying for you and your team. It can help to foster stronger relationships, encourage motivation and ensure that your best employees stay with you for longer.

Mentoring is good practice within a company and is great for increasing staff retention. Don't just take my word for it. A study by the Chartered Management Institute in the UK among managers, for instance, found that the biggest threat to business in 2011 is a lack of skills among employees. Now that's an issue that you can do something about – if you mentor your staff well! A third of managers cite that they plan to put more time and effort into coaching and mentoring their team in 2011 as a result, and you should too. It makes sense all round.

A study by the University of Pennsylvania (of more than 1,000 employees in a large tech company over five years) says it best. It found that those in the company's mentor programme were promoted at six times the rate of their non-mentored counterparts. Not to mention that their retention rate was 72 per cent compared to their obviously unhappier (and un-mentored) colleagues (49 per cent).

That's a pretty convincing argument!

Before we even begin to discuss how to mentor a team, however, we should make sure we're on the same page as to what a mentor actually does.

It's simple really; a good mentor helps their employee with planning, feedback and education, keeping them on track as they go through the learning process. Whether it's helping them to plan deadlines and schedules, agreeing timelines, providing a gentle push forward when they struggle on tasks or reminding them of the bigger picture and their own goals if they become demotivated, a mentor's help can be vital.

For the mentee, it's a rare chance to learn from the best; even if you personally can't help them in every situation, you will probably know the people that can.

A quick word to the wise – while having a mentor is great for morale and career progression, don't mollycoddle your reports. At some point they are going to have to stand on their own two feet and you want to encourage them to do that from the beginning. You want them to know that there is someone rooting for them, but at the end of the day, the success has to be theirs alone.

So, How Can you Mentor?

I've found the following tips work extremely well when it comes to mentoring staff:

Listen to them: Be there for your mentees when they need you; this doesn't mean you have to drop everything when they call but you should make the time to actually mentor them. There's nothing worse than an out-of-reach mentor. Whether it's a face-to-face chat or over the telephone, your mentee needs to know that they can speak to you if there's a problem.

It doesn't have to be you: Some companies have a formal mentoring scheme whereby all new recruits are matched up with a more experienced employee who shows them the ropes, passes on their knowledge and generally eases their progression into the team. If you don't have a scheme like this, think about introducing it. It can be formal or informal, in which case ask for employee mentoring volunteers. You can put the new employee with a more senior member of staff and ask them to look after them; just make sure you check in on their progress from time to time.

Let them make mistakes: When you mentor someone, it's natural to want to prevent them from making mistakes. But as I said in our delegation section, it's important to take a step back and let them fail every now and again. It's how we learn. If you try to take over whenever an employee seems to be struggling, the only message you'll be passing on is that they are incompetent and they'll soon stop trying to learn and grow. Keep an eye on their progress informally – walking past their desk and asking them, "Hey, how's it going? Any questions?" is a good opening gambit. Of course, it's not always easy to explain to your own boss why mistakes are being made. Hopefully you'll have a strong mentoring scheme where any mistakes will be caught before they go too far down the line; in which case, you may not need to inform your boss at all. If you do need to tell the boss about mistakes, however, make sure you have already found a solution to the problem at hand, or better yet, put it into practice; that way, you can show that you are taking responsibility, are on top of the situation and have rectified it. If all else fails, remind the boss firmly that he or she needs to trust you and gave you the job for a reason. They now need to stand back and let you do it.

Talk to them about their goals and look for any ways that you can help the employee to reach them. Act as a sounding board.

Don't keep all the good stuff to yourself: A good mentor is selfless. If there's a part of the job that seems fun or will let an employee shine in the company – perhaps it's being photographed for a charity drive or giving a presentation at the local school – don't always keep it for yourself. Send a trusted employee to do it for you; spread the love around. The affirmation the employee gets will do wonders for their morale.

Invite them to sit in on meetings, interviews or important events within the company to get a wider view of why you do things. Take the time to explain your thinking afterwards.

Give praise where it's due: This is where a great many managers fall down. We can handle the negative reprimands when we need to, but we forget to pass along the congratulations when an employee does something well. As a society, we're often so focused on dealing with problems that we overlook the good work that goes on or take it for granted. As such, walking around saying "good job" or giving someone a pat on the back can often feel false, if for no other reason than we have to remind ourselves to do it. Novice managers or those who struggle with communication may feel awkward when giving compliments, but here's a tough lesson for you: get over it. Forget about your own feelings and think about the employee's. The good news is that the more you give praise, the more natural it will start to feel. As a good rule of thumb, always give praise when someone has gone above and beyond the call of duty; show them that their extra work or initiative is recognised.

Don't step over the line: While you want to be a supportive and respectful mentor, don't confuse it with being friends. You may still have to reprimand that employee at a later date, so never put yourself in a position where it is impossible to do that. Avoid sharing embarrassing personal stories or health concerns that show you in a less than professional light, for instance, or getting raging drunk with them every Friday night. If you haven't already, read our section on Can you be Friends with your Employees?

Likewise, don't try to mould them into a model of yourself. It's tempting to assume your mentee should follow in your footsteps and do things in the same manner as you do; it can even be disappointing if they don't. Keep your mind open, however; the company may benefit from a new approach. As long as the work gets done well and your mentee seems to be progressing, that's all you can ask for.

Finally, a quick heartfelt word – **never be afraid to mentor**. You should never be reluctant to share knowledge that can benefit the business as a whole. Remember that your staff look to you for guidance; they will take their steer from you and your attitude. If you are, or become, the kind of boss that jealously guards your knowledge, afraid to let other people share it for fear that they may be a threat to your job, that's the company ethos that will ensue. And that's the sort of company you don't want – and the type of business that people don't want to work for.

Chapter 4: Resolving Conflicts

Jeanette and Charles are biologists. They were chosen to work on a research project together. Right from the start, Jeanette decided her colleague was morose, and didn't have the qualities necessary to work effectively as part of a team, on a demanding project.

After two weeks, Jeanette was at the end of her rope. Not only was Charles as socially inept as a block of wood, he also refused to share his scientific data with her. The atmosphere in the small lab, where they spent entire days together, became unbearable. Jeanette found it harder and harder to sleep, and her work began to suffer. She broke out in pimples, although she'd never had acne in her life before. The dermatologist she consulted immediately concluded that her skin disorder was the result of stress.

Finally, after an out and out argument with Charles, Jeanette decided to get to the bottom of things. She discreetly questioned other colleagues who knew Charles, and tried to find out about his past behavior. And each time he became negative with her, she made sure to write down the circumstances that provoked the conflict.

This is a question Jeanette asked herself, once she discovered the underlying causes behind Charles' negative behavior, and was able to identify her own role in the situation.

If you find yourself facing a person who, like Charles, has been embittered by the vicissitudes of life - personal disappointments, frustrated ambitions, professional conflicts, etc. - it is possible to overcome the barrier between you without damaging either the other person or yourself, and at the same time assert yourself to advantage.

Here's what to do:

Ask for a meeting with the other person. If necessary, set a definite time and place. Try to make sure you won't be interrupted, and show the other person that you take the problem seriously.

Start the discussion by stating that you believe the situation between you isn't clear. Something's definitely wrong.

Wait for the person's reaction.

Depending on the way the person reacts - or doesn't react - to your overtures, determine what type of "difficult" person you're dealing with.

Be diplomatic! For example, after Jeanette set up a meeting with Charles, she didn't come right out and say, "Oh, I know all about what happened with your job transfer, and about your insecurity because you didn't go to a great school!"

Above all, don't be condescending or arrogant. And finally, something we can't seem to repeat often enough - DON'T TRY TO READ THE OTHER PERSON'S MIND. There's nothing more exasperating. How would you feel if someone was constantly doing it to you?

Example:

Here's how Jeanette got the conversation rolling:

"I feel there's some tension between us, and it's beginning to affect our work. I don't have as much experience as you do, and I was hoping to learn, a lot and improve my methods by working with you. But that's not happening. Do you think we're just incompatible? Is it the mistakes I've made that are bothering you? Is it the methods I use? I'd like to know what you think about it."

Stop trying to change other people

This is probably one of the most important keys to success in the area of human relations. We seem to possess an extraordinary capacity for creating illusions about the people around us, and especially about those we love. We often love people despite their faults, but only because we hope that someday they'll change and conform more closely to our desired image of them.

We spend years trying to get someone to change the way we want them to, until the day comes when we realise that changing another person is beyond our powers, especially if the change we are striving to produce runs counter to that person's own will.

When that day comes, we either start loving the person for who s/he is, or we stop loving them altogether - and that's where the danger lies.

Human beings can change

This is not to deny that people have the capacity to change.

It is evident that every human being evolves throughout the course of his / her existence. The environment causes us to change, as does the exercise of individual will, and this continues right up to very old age.

But it is during the first twelve years of life that people are most malleable. And yet, even during this first phase of existence, we have the utmost difficulty getting our children to conform to our wishes.

It goes without saying that once a person reaches adulthood, his / her evolution is almost completely beyond the conscious control of anyone else, under normal circumstances.

Try to remember the last time you had an unpleasant or painful encounter with someone, and said to yourself, "If only he were less uptight!" or "If only he were a little more tolerant..." or "If only old people were less demanding..." or "If only my kids were less selfish..." and so on.

Our wishes are not reality

Our error consists of believing that others should conform to our desires, and when they don't live up to our expectations, we blame them for it. We label them difficult or intolerant, selfish or overly demanding, indecisive or vain, etc.

The important thing is to realise that we're dealing with a real human being, and that every person has his/her qualities and faults. Other people are not projections of our imagination - we can't eliminate aspects of their personality that do not live up to our expectations, nor can we give them qualities we think they should possess.

That's why I'm so pleased whenever someone says, "You're disappointing me." To me, this means that the person hasn't been in touch with who I really am, but with a projection of who they think I am - in other words, with themselves. Imagine all the time we waste being a screen for other people's projections!

So the intelligent thing to do is obviously to become conscious of the reality of people around us, both of those who please us, and those who don't. We should also know that we can contribute significantly to their happiness and self fulfilment, on condition that they wish us to do so.

You can influence people's attitudes

While you may do your utmost to improve a situation between yourself and a "difficult" person, you should under no circumstances attempt to modify that person's personality. You will not succeed, and in any case it won't be of any use.

The only thing you can do is modify a person's attitude toward you. It is towards this goal that you should direct all your efforts.

You do more for the person this way than by trying to change his / her personality, and make the person easier to live with, from your point of view, of course.

By bringing the problem or conflict that is poisoning your relationship out in the open, you help the other person see him / herself more clearly, just as you've been able to see yourself better because of the efforts you've been making.

And it is by becoming aware of the forces, the ambitions, the desires and repulsions that make us act in certain ways, that enable us to take control of our lives, assert ourselves and attain fulfilment.

Distance yourself

When faced with a difficult relationship, we tend to get deeply involved. We lose all sense of objectivity. Our day to day lives are soon affected, as we become preoccupied with the problem. We may even become obsessed by the difficult person in question, and the problems s/he is causing.

This is what happened at first to Jeaneatte, our biologist. Overwhelmed by her problems with Charles, she became unable to sleep, couldn't do her work properly, until she took hold of herself and analysed the situation as if she were an outside observer.

But keeping your distance from someone who exerts a strong influence is easier said than done. Difficult people seem to know how to trigger negative emotions - they always seem to know just what to say or do to make us upset.

Adopt a strategy and apply it

In your exchanges with difficult people, there are really only two types of strategy to choose from. Either you get involved in a power struggle, with the aim of coming out on top. Or you look for a way to achieve satisfying results while taking the other person's needs into account.

The upper hand

As we've seen in section before, there are different types of "difficult" people, so it follows that our strategy will depend on the type of attack that you are subjected to.

For example, if you're dealing with a negative type, who gradually manages to intoxicate your mind with measured doses of pessimism, you'd be less inclined to get into a power struggle situation than if you were dealing with a "steamroller" type.

When we look at the world around us, we see that the struggle for survival seems to resemble a frantic competition, where the big fish swallow up the little fish, and the strong dominate the weak. So there's a great temptation to consider our relations with difficult people as a struggle, where the only aim is to gain the upper hand.

However, you've probably noticed that in the preceding parts we have avoided suggesting that gaining the upper hand become the main objective of your training in interprets on all relations.

Avoid win - lose situations

The reason for this approach is that wherever you have a win - lose situation, the loser will not rest until s/he has found some way of getting revenge. We could even qualify this reaction as "natural" since it is so common.

But if you think about it, you'll see that although the animal kingdom does rely on the balance created by the strong devouring the weak, nowhere in nature do we see a weak animal waiting patiently for years, and sometimes even for generations if necessary, in order to reverse the roles and exact revenge on another animal, for a past humiliation.

This is a characteristically human trait, which, as we know, results in all kinds of disasters - wars, famine, repression, needless destruction, and so on.

This is why our recommendations are aimed at "restoring communication at the point where it broke down" and "defining your position, as well as that of the other person, if necessary." Not letting someone walk all over you doesn't necessarily mean dominating that person. It means not letting another person dominate you and, based on this affirmation of self, doing something constructive about the situation.

Win-win strategy and the game of life

Another way to approach our relations with others is to try to produce a situation that satisfies both our needs, as well as the other person's.

There are people for whom we feel no special sympathy, who surprise us with the generous and unsolicited things they do for us. Each time we feel like a winner in our relations with them, we are, consciously or unconsciously, scoring a golden point in their favour. The day may come when they do something that tips the scales, this time in a positive sense, and we find ourselves experiencing an immense feeling of gratitude towards them.

A narrow view of life could give us the impression that nature is nothing more than a huge battlefield. But science has shown us that, above all, nature is a study in balance. If a species disappears because of a predator's success, the predator will also disappear, for lack of food.

The more progress we make in understanding the universe, the more we discover that everything is somehow related to everything else. Winning by forcing someone else to lose out ultimately means setting yourself up to lose out as well. That's the way the game of life works. We're all in the same boat, and if I make a hole in the hull because I want you to sink, I'm eventually going to sink too.

In fact, what is occurring now, thanks to developments in science and communication, is a mutation of consciousness which is unprecedented in the history of humanity. We are discovering that the choice of being a winner by making others losers, is not a real choice at all. The real choice is that either we both win together, or we both lose together. This is the only alternative we have. And that's why we must develop a win - win attitude, to the point where it becomes a reflex, in almost all situations.

When we're dealing with likable, nice, easy-going people, it happens naturally. We find certain people "disarming" and couldn't imagine doing anything to harm them, probably because we'd feel too guilty afterwards.

On the other hand, when we have to deal with difficult persons, things become a lot harder, probably because we feel they have wronged us in some way, and we wish to punish them for it.

We have the choice

However, even in these types of situations we have the choice of creating a relationship based on force and domination, a relationship which is bound to fail eventually, or to look for a way to satisfy both parties.

When faced with a difficult person, you have to be very clear on what strategy you intend using: are you going to try and crush the other person in order to experience the pleasure (albeit very temporary) of victory or revenge, without thinking about the price you'll have to pay later for your elation?

Or are you going to protect yourself first, and then look for ways to establish a constructive dialogue?

These two fundamental options are always available to you. The only variable, therefore, is your choice of approach.

Become aware of negative interaction

The main problem with applying a win-win approach is that the negativity which characterises the communication can easily engender more negativity in you. This is what is meant by negative interaction - the old vicious circle.

They're sometimes impossible to avoid. We're so upset and exasperated that any possibility of improving the situation, or bringing it to a positive conclusion, seems very remote.

When you're the target of anger, slander, and injustice, it can be all but impossible to control yourself, and not react in kind.

However, if you wish to assert yourself, improve the situation, and help the other person all at the same time, then you have no choice. You must learn to control the way you react, in order to break the vicious circle and set up a cycle of positive interaction in its place.

What you're being asked to do, in order to defuse conflict situations and start communicating with difficult persons, is to respond to their anger with patience, to their disdain with respect, and to their harmful intentions with benevolence.

If you think that this is a superhuman task, reserved for angels and saints, then you will inevitably perpetuate the cycles of misunderstanding and violence you encounter. But rest assured, although reacting in this way may be reserved for "evolved" persons, it is by no means beyond the reach of the average human being.

The simple fact that you've read this far is sufficient proof that developing such reflexes would not present much of a problem for you. All you have to do is practice the exercises suggested a little later on.

Above all, strive for positive interaction

Here's some good news: in the same way that negative attracts negative, positive attracts positive. The hard thing to do is reverse the current, and we'll be looking here at a few methods for effecting this change.

We've already stressed the importance of not responding to aggression with aggression. We must refer to it again, since it is the cornerstone of achieving any significant changes in your conflicting or difficult relationships.

We analysed how difficult persons seem to have the capacity for bringing out the worst in us, for bringing us down to their level, so that we find ourselves doing the very same things we've been criticising them for doing! However, don't forget that as difficult as a person may be, s/he is still capable of responding positively to the right kind of stimulus; everyone (almost) possesses all the necessary resources for becoming an open, positive and communicative person.

To start the process, you must first categorically refuse to participate in any destructive games. Then, when attempts to involve you in such games cease, you can start your work being the engine that pulls the relationship in a positive direction.

Get rid of all the garbage and junk that is weighing you down. Start collecting "golden points" in all your relationships. Create conditions for positive interaction, for "virtuous" circles instead of vicious ones. I guarantee your life will undergo a miraculous change for the better.

Chapter 5: Disrespectful Employees

Who they are: These are the employees who answer back to the boss or show aggression in the workplace. They may walk away from you as you are talking to them, or talk over you while you are trying to speak to them or someone else. They may even tell you that they refuse to listen to you or to do what you ask of them. This is potentially one of the hardest employee problems to deal with as it can drain the manager's energy and create a culture of confrontation. While some feedback and discussion between the manager and the team is a good thing – a good manager always listens to his or her team and then makes his or her own decisions – aggression or an argumentative employee is not.

New managers in particular may find it hard to deal with an employee who questions their directions publicly or, even worse, refuses to do what is asked of them. It can be just as difficult to deal with aggressive loud employees who antagonise the workforce and demand attention. So just how should you deal with a disrespectful or aggressive employee?

What to do:

It can be difficult to know how to handle an employee who disrespects or shouts at you in front of other people. The key is to tackle it immediately and to stay calm; a slanging match between you and the employee in front of the rest of the workforce will only make things worse. At the same time, you need to show that such behaviour will not be tolerated. Take a deep breath, stay calm and tell the employee that you want to listen to his or her concerns but you cannot do that while he or she is shouting at you. Tell them you will speak to them about their concerns privately. Keeping a level head will hopefully help to defuse the tension; at the very least, it will show the rest of the workforce that you are handling the situation professionally.

If you have to deal with someone who answers you back or deliberately tries to belittle you, the first thing you need to do is to have a conversation in private. Start by setting the ground rules - that shouting will not be allowed and the employee will not interrupt you when you are speaking. Likewise, promise that you will listen to their concerns as well. You want the employee in question to talk to you honestly, as opposed to being defensive or arguing. Have examples of their responses on hand in case they try to deny it.

Make it obvious that you are curious about what the employee is intending by their behaviour; what message is he or she trying to convey? Are they resentful and if so, why? What is the problem? If this behaviour is recent, what has changed between you? This demonstrates that you really want to get to the bottom of the problem.

If they are willing to talk, listen to their answers without feeling the need to defend yourself; there may be relevant points about your own behaviour that you could take on board.

Hopefully this conversation will assess whether the perceived slights are deliberate, a result of miscommunication or a reaction to your own behaviour to him or her. The key to the meeting is to end it with an agreement of how you will work together in a positive way.

Let's take a quick look at how your dialogue could start. You should ideally have this conversation at the first available opportunity to do so in private, after any incident. If the situation has arisen slowly and over time, however, take the opportunity to first come up with a concrete list of examples of the employee's unacceptable behaviour in case they try to deny it. This is particularly useful if there hasn't been any obvious blow out but the disrespect has been more insidious. If you have line managers working for you, ask for their feedback before the meeting as well.

Manager: "Jack, I want to talk to you about some troubling behaviour that I've noticed recently. I feel like I'm being disrespected and I can sense that something has changed recently between us. I'd like to give you the chance to discuss why that could be?"

Employee: "I don't know what you mean."

Manager: "Really? Well, just yesterday you refused to do the work that I had assigned to you, while the day before you walked away from me when I was talking to you. I think it's obvious there are some issues here and I'd like to get to the bottom of what they are. I need your help to do that. I don't know if there's something bothering you or if you feel I could be doing more to support you in your work, but please let me know if that is the case. Did you feel it was inappropriate of me to ask you to if the project was going to be finished on time?"

Employee: "My projects are always finished on time."

Manager: "OK, so I'm not allowed to ask? Tell me, whose responsibility should it be to keep everyone up-to-date on this? Should it be mine to ask you or yours to keep me informed? How would you feel if you were the line manager and a subordinate responded to you that way in front of other members of the team?"

Employee: "I guess I wouldn't like it."

Manager: "OK, so this is your chance to talk to me. Help me understand. What would you like me to know about you and working with you that would make your job easier?"

[Discussion continues...]

If the problem isn't so much that the employee answers you back in particular, but that they are generally aggressive, demanding and loud, alienating the entire workforce, you may need to take a different tack. First and foremost, try to understand what is driving the person's behaviour. Often the employee in question is looking to be recognised and rewarded and this is their clumsy way of doing it; hopefully you are praising your team when it is deserved already, if not you should start.

If the problem remains however, you have to tackle it, if for no other reason than aggressive people ruin cooperation and dominate the workforce. No one wants to help someone who won't listen, talks over them or down to them, is a know-it-all and is often rude and sarcastic. Likewise, the employee in question may well be spreading negativity to other members of staff, who may or may not take their side. Remember, the employee can say whatever he or she wants out of your earshot; you don't have the same luxury as you can't talk about one employee with another. You don't know therefore what your other employees are being exposed to.

If you need to talk to aggressive people – whether it's about their aggression or the fact that they haven't done the work they promised – here are a few tips on how to do so with discretion:

First, let them vent. Aggressive people are often angry.

Listen to them and show that you are listening. While it may be hard to get a word in edgeways, chip in with words such as "Yes,", "No", "I don't agree", "I agree" etc... For all their domineering, people don't usually listen to aggressive people; the fact that you are will slow them down a bit.

When they finally finish venting, clarify their main point to show them you were listening. Don't get bogged down with all their other complaints; address only the key issue at hand. Don't be afraid to tell them if you disagree with any of their points. Hold your ground; don't give in to their bullying. If they start to get angry or aggressive again, say their name over and over again until they stop to listen. If they do finally stop ranting, speak calmly and make sure you have understood their complaints. If they walk away because they are not getting their way, however, they have upped the ante and now you need to do so too, via your progressive discipline.

Be professional at all times; don't wind them up or anger them for the sake of it. Stay calm.

Finally, indicate what you would like to see them doing more or less of. State clearly what you expect from them and get their agreement to make one or two key changes.

If this doesn't work, don't be afraid to fire the aggressor. Sometimes you simply can't afford to have one person who disrupts the team so much.

Chapter 6: Find A Common Thread And Sew It Up!

Sometimes we all have something in common with another person. An important strength in relationship building is having a commonality with someone else. One way to tell is by looking at the person's work area. There are usually clues that tell a little about a person's background. Photos, memorabilia, knickknacks, these are things that can tell a lot about a person. When you get right down to it, every friend you have has something in common with you. Where did you meet your best friend? Some we met at school, some we met at work, in our neighborhood, through another friend...

Okay, so you don't particularly want to be friends with this coworker. Well, being friends at work is a lot better than being miserable, isn't it? And if it is only for 8 hours a day, 5 days a week, it certainly is doable. Nothing says that you have to hang out with this person after work or on weekends. Be friendly! (You never know, this person might turn out to be your best friend.)

Finding that common thread can bring about that connection that 2 people need to communicate. Look for photos of kids—grandkids—pets—hobbies. Somewhere along the line, you are going to find a commonality. When that happens, the door will open. Then use that thread to keep the lines of communication open. Compliments go a long way to starting that conversation on a positive note. Starting positively usually sets the tone for the interaction.

If we are looking at the neighbor, look for that commonality—gardens, pets, cars. Use these topics to strike up a conversation with your neighbor. Ask him/her about their garden—how do they keep the pests away? What kind of fertilizer do they use? Most people, even grouchy old people, like to talk about the things that they love. And older people love to give advice—even if you don't really care about the topic, showing interest will give both of you a reason to smile and say hi to each other. It will open a line of communication that can lead to both of you being good neighbors.

It is worth the effort to find ways to coexist with other people. You never know when that person just might save your life or just be there when you need someone. Stranger things have happened.

Chapter 7: The Power Of Words In Dealing With A Difficult Person

Mastering the right word to apply at the right time is an advantage over any form of situation. When dealing with a difficult person, the choice of words that you employ counts and matter a lot. It is more of overcoming evil with goodness.

Words go a long way. Words are very powerful. Words can cause you a big problem, and at the same time, solve or prevent bigger problems.

A wise person is known by his words. A fool also is recognized by his words too. And one thing you must know is that the words from the mouth are like a screen revealing the state of the heart.

A wise person is known with his carefully chosen words in times of provocation while a fool is known by the multitudes of carelessly chosen words. One strange being that once walked on the surface of this earth said- "out of the abundance of the heart the mouth speaks".

Words carry power and can be channeled to bring about any cause. The Bible says; life and death are in the power of the tongue. This means your words can make you or mar you.

However, relating the power of words to the strategies of dealing with a difficult person is very compulsory. Like I said in chapter one about what in discovered concerning my room-mate; that after my discoveries about how he takes jokes, I had to tame my jokes and carefully choose my words when trying to converse or joke with him. Like I said, it really solved a lot of problems.

Your choice of words in any form of relationship has a lot to do not to talk of dealing with someone difficult. If you must maintain a cordial, smooth and joyous relationship with anyone, your tone in communication and choice of words have important roles to play. If there must be a lot of carefulness in choosing words to deal with ordinary people, how much more a difficult person?

"A soft answer turneth away wrath but grievous words stir up anger" – These words are words of wisdom form a popular ancient king.

When you observe closely this proverb very well, you will notice he said **"stir up anger"** and **"not cause to be angry"**. This vividly means the person in question is dealing with an angry fellow and not a cool headed person. And his answer or words must be soft or carefully chosen in order to avoid or quench the anger. So, if you must win a heart over or overcome a difficult situation, your words must be fire quenching and anger avoiding.

Words are very powerful. The way you use it will determine the result you will get.

WHAT ARE OTHER FACTS CONCERNING WORDS?

The whole world was created and put in place by words. God spoke the universe in to existence.

As great and might as the sun is, it is an end product of words from the mouth of the almighty.

Words carry potent power that builds or demolishes.

A relationship of 30 or 50 years can be ruined in minutes if words are wrongly used.

If not for wrong usage of words, most problems that mankind is facing might not have surfaced at all. Also if words can be aligned used rightly, most of our problems could have disappeared.

Words are very fragile. They are like eggs. Once they slip off the tongue carelessly, they are no longer reparable again.

Words are also like the spit from the mouth. Once you spit a dangerous word, there is no way you can swallow it back.

Silence isn't the absence of words but the ability to control words or tame them.

Silence is the best answer for a fool but right use of words can develop a fool into a wise man.

Words can either make you or mare you.

Words are like seeds. If you sow the right ones, you will get good results. If you sow the wrongs ones, you will get negative results.

Words for the mouth of a wise man are like sword. They can penetrate to deepest part of the body, touching the heart and healing the soul.

If you need confession of any kind from any mind, the power of your words will determine if you will get it or not. Word have the power to draw out hidden secrets of the heart bring them to light plainly.

Your word will tell if someone difficult will change towards you or not.

Words are the bloodline of communication.

Your tone matters a lot when uttering words.

Then the last but not the least, you must be able to master the power of right words. You should be able to know what to apply and how to apply them in facing any challenge of situation.

HOW DO YOU USE THE POWER OF WORDS IN DEALING WITH DIFFICULT PEOPLE?

Make sure you avoid talking too much in the person's presence. Always learn how to be reserved.

When it is time to talk, carefully choose your words and don't rush into pouring out words.

Convince the person that you can keep secrets and you are capable of handling any situation.

Mater the habit of saying "I am sorry" even if you have not really committed an offence.

When you have just offended or you need to challenge the person, in your own wisdom, carefully rehearse on how you will launch it and the tone you will apply.

Be slow to speak and be quick to hear.

Observe the mood and atmosphere before going make complains or say your mind.

Praying to God concerning the person's heart towards you is also using the power of words indirectly.

Don't take serious matters with the hands of levity in the person's presence. There is time for everything.

Always try to observe the look and reactions when you use some certain words. This will help you to know which words you should do away with or the similar ones you can apply when the reaction is positive.

I f you must start any conversation with a superior or boss, carefully notice the mood and the atmosphere. Then ask for permission before starting.

Let your words be so powerful positively that even when you leave it will still ring bell in the heart of your receiver.

At times, you need to be silent and mutter no words just for peace to reign. It is also a power of words. It shows your ability to take control.

And lastly; do not report a difficult person to another person. Doing that will might worsen the case. One good way to do it is to report a difficult person to himself or herself.

All these are ways in which one can use the power of words to handle a difficult person.

Chapter 8: Practical Examples On How To Deal With Difficult People

Difficult people are not impossible people

Practical Examples on How to Deal with Difficult

People

Difficult people are not impossible people. You can talk sense into them, if you know how.

There are ways to get them to stop being obnoxious and to listen for even just a while - and this moment is crucial. You must put in your best rebuttal and convince them to put down their defenses, or else lose them forever.

Difficult people are real people, so dealing with them must be practical and out of common sense.

Here are some tried and tested approaches to capture their attention:

A Difficult Self

As a Chinese proverb goes, the first enemy to defeat is you. A Jewish proverb mentions that conquering the self is greater than conquering a city.

If anyone fails to conquer the self, says the proverb, he is like a city whose walls have collapsed.

When the self is controlled, any difficult person becomes a piece of cake. So be disciplined to ignore the cravings of your ego.

Practice the 7 practical steps and the 12 pointers in the previous chapter.

When you have ascertained that you are not a difficult person yourself, you have every right, and the strength to come to the rescue of one who is.

A Difficult Spouse

Unless you are contemplating divorce, your spouse is a lifetime partner.

It's easy to give up on a difficult spouse, but doing so may mean you are a difficult person too.

Re-marrying may either get you a new difficult partner, or a helpless victim.

Pressures melt away when you are a good listener to any complainant.

Often, pressures need release.

Listening to your spouse complain while you keep mum and sincere will do wonders for both of you.

Difficulties rise when both parties complain and no issue is brought to light.

To bring light, both parties cannot be stuck in the darkness. One must provide the spark. If you opt not to be the difficult party and just listen intently, you're already providing that spark.

Though a heart-to-heart talk cannot pay pending bills and buy groceries, it can clear minds to think positively for a temporary alternative or refuge, if not a lasting solution.

Clear minds are necessary when there's no money in sight to answer financial woes, or in any dilemma for that matter.

Aside from lending an open ear, a little gift won't hurt.

Buy your spouse a little something or treat yourselves to a refreshing drink or snack after the heat dies down.

Best of all, heal wounds by passionate love-making. Love conquers all.

When a partner is difficult because of a third party, you should strive to be the exact opposite of your spouse.

Opposites attract.

You can still save the marriage by not adding fuel to the fire. You can actually pour water on it through your calmness and composure.

Should worse comes to worst, you might lose your spouse to a third party, but not your dignity.

Just imagine the agony of losing both.

Difficult Parents

Parents can be demanding.

The pressure can come from a frustrated ambition they want their children to fulfill for them.

It may be an ambition they have planned for their children, which the latter may reject.

It may also be their desire for their children to perform greater than the children of a neighbor, friend, or relative.

It may also be a work or money related pressure.

Whatever the reason parents become difficult, their children carry the brunt of the problem.

If neglected, the kids will likely carry the problem with them as they grow and it will become a vicious cycle passed on to succeeding generations.

Grandparents can play a special role in neutralizing the pressure suffered by the children, but the best antidote is for them to be agreeable.

This can strengthen the character of the children as they grow.

Lacking this may frustrate them and the children may become withdrawn.

Having a strong character is healthy, but being withdrawn has some temporary setbacks.

However, any setback can be resolved when children opt to be different from their difficult parents as they grow up, without detesting them.

At the right age, when children develop right judgment, they can begin to deal positively with difficult parents.

They can start by being more intimate with their parents, by showing more concern and love, and by being more sincere and thoughtful.

Remember, opposites attract.

They can show more respect for the opinions and feelings of the parents, even though the parents may not reciprocate.

With such contrast, the faulty parents will slowly detect the difference and realize the wrong.

Rebelling against parents will only make the parents worse.

Difficult parents see control as a first and last resort. And when you fight difficulty with difficulty, it's difficult to resolve.

Difficulty cannot be countered unless one party gives in.

When your parents start to see your good attitude despite their unfair treatment, you become a precious gem to them.

They will see that you are dependable and trustworthy.

You can then begin to share your own dreams and ambitions, or the pressure you get from their insistence on their plans for you.

Few responsible parents can resist a good child. They may do so for a while, but they will give in soon.

Remember to always be tender and polite in your conversations with your parents.

Even if they remain difficult, stay cool.

Even if you get turned down often, pursue goodness.

Water has sculptured landforms through the years, and can destroy the hardest steel.

Difficult Children

If you are a parent experiencing problems with difficult children, then this section would be of great significance.

Before dealing with your difficult children, ask yourself first where your youngsters got the attitude. Check yourself and your spouse. Make sure your children didn't acquire the attitude from either of you.

If your children did acquire their behavior from any of you, deal with the source first.

After the attitude has been dealt with in you or in your spouse, then the children come next.

Children can also become difficult by lack of proper discipline.

The parents may not be difficult, but the difficult attitude may develop in the children when the parents give in to everything that their children demand.

In other words, the children would become spoiled brats.

Then again, children can become difficult because of wrong discipline.

Harsh and cruel discipline can seriously scar the emotional development of children and may cause them to develop selfish animosity towards others.

Difficult children are easy to deal with if you start disciplining them early.

Right training at an early age guarantees excellent results. Children will almost never depart from the system you have ingrained in them if you start teaching them at the earliest stages.

Take walking as an example. We train children to walk after a few months from their birth. Otherwise, it may adversely affect their way of walking if you delay.

If you notice a difficult attitude in your children, make sure to deal with it right away. But make sure you do it right.

Don't be cruel or harsh. This will only aggravate the situation and

you will end up being a difficult parent.

The safest way to start is to make sure you practice the 7 practical

ways and 12 pointers explained earlier here.

If you are a gentle, loving, but firm parent, dealing with difficult

children is peanuts.

When correcting your children, explain to them that the discipline

is for their own benefit, and it is out of love.

Again, love conquers all.

Make sure the scolding and disciplining is done in private. If you

embarrass children in public you push them to become rebellious.

Avoid pacifying your kids, especially those having tantrums, by

giving them what they want.

The impression this makes is that a difficult attitude is rewarded,

and that difficult children always get what they want.

The right way to pacify grumpy kids is to assure them of your love, and that the discipline you are giving them is an act of love.

Embracing or kissing children will help will drive this point home.

Children are rewarded more by the tender touch of parents, as

adults are touched more by the affection of those they love.

Some people refrain from disciplining their difficult children, or

simply pretend the problem does not exist, because they think doing so is showing love for them.

If they grow up with the difficult attitude, it will carve out a

miserable life for them and those around them, and it all fall back on the parents.

Real love is helping the children grow up loving others as well.

It should be stressed that just because some kids become

mischievous or naughty, it does not mean they are already difficult.

Children are apt to be so. They are children.

Children are difficult when they demand others to recognize that

they alone are right.

It is one thing for kids to think they're right; it's quite another for

them to demand others that they alone are right.

Difficult Siblings

Difficult brothers or sisters can mar your image and the image of your family.

Now, before anything, make sure you yourself are not difficult. After you are cleared of this, then you can begin to examine and

deal with difficult siblings.

Difficult siblings are so mostly because of rivalry.

When parents or people exercising authority over them show

favorites, or when there is rivalry in courtship, siblings can become difficult.

This is especially true to their fellow siblings.

And it is especially true when their fellow siblings succumb to the

pressure.

Often, these are overt and covert pressures combined, working

within and without. These combined pressures are usually prominent in sibling rivalries.

Your first and last line of defense is humility.

Quit trying to prove anything about yourself and start honestly

praising your difficult siblings.

Even if things seem to favor you more than your siblings, stress

your equality.

We all have positive and negative traits; it so happens that your

positive qualities mostly outshine your negatives, and that your time to be in the limelight seems scheduled in the present.

Tell them that everyone has a day in that limelight and theirs may

come soon.

Once your siblings see that you pose no threat to them, the rivalry ends and harmony starts to evolve. The pressure subsides

markedly, and may even die once the threat perception is totally dismissed.

LOT will be at an all-time high because everything, even tight

situations, will become tolerable in the absence of any threat or rivalry.

When a challenge occurs, it won't be a contest of "who's going to

solve it first and solve it better" anymore, but it's going to be a "let's solve it for the family" thing.

Difficult Relatives

Difficult relatives do not pose much of a problem because you're likely to see them only in family reunions --- except if you live in

said relatives' house.

In this case, you can apply the strategies to counter difficult

siblings as explained above.

Your first and last line of defense is humility.

You may also establish clearly that you are not a threat to your

relatives. Prove that you are an ally, not an adversary.

A little research on your relatives' background might help. Find the

reasons why they ended up difficult. But do the study secretly;

don't go around asking their families and friends regarding them.

Whatever you find out will help you in figuring out ways to relate

with them.

If the cause of their being difficult is a result of pressure from:

a) Parents - They need support in pleasing their parents. b) Siblings - They need to receive honest praises and to

have a positive outlook to neutralize sibling rivalry.

c) Friends - They have to eliminate their low self-esteem.

Perk up their spirits.

d) Bosses - Treat them out on weekends. Try to help them

look for better jobs, if they are constantly complaining about their work.

e) Themselves - Be patient and show sincerity.

Act natural. The last thing difficult people want is to get help from other people. They think they know everything and that they are always right.

Let's look at a sample situation:

All his close friends have found their respective girlfriends and

your difficult relative still has not.

He begins to feel the pressure and he opts to pass it on to you -

because you're just a free boarder in his house, and it's incumbent

upon the "master" to pick on his "slave."

To ease the situation, don't start telling him how handsome he

actually is, and that the pretty girls are just too blind to see that.

Start small by appreciating his new haircut, his new shoes that fit

him well, or perhaps his good penmanship.

Appreciate his books or collection of films or music.

He may react negatively, and even besmirch you for being nosy

about his things. But just keep on, and make each appreciation

more polite and sincere, until he realizes that you are his ally.

When he realizes that and starts to trust you, neutralize the pressure

by stressing other things that give self-confidence other than having a girlfriend: Like having a pure heart, for instance.

Difficult Friends

Many among us are often closer to our friends than to our relatives.

Difficult relatives are nothing compared to difficult friends.

If you get caught up with such friends, rather than dilly-dallying

and working out a painstaking process of convincing them that you are an ally, give it to them straight. That's what friends are for. The painful words of friends are better than the flattery of fools.

Tell them how you actually feel. If you can't tell them that, they're

not really your friends. They're just acquaintances.

Real friends are often reflections of another you. They can even be

regarded as your alter egos.

Acquaintances are those you know, for a long time or recently, but

whom you still sometimes distrust, or size up. They are those people who you can live without, though you also care for them.

But remember that as you deal with difficult friends, make sure

you exercise some measure of tolerance for their imperfections.

Give them enough time to adjust.

Some healing processes take a long time: When difficult friends

get hurt, the harm is sometimes skin-deep, but oftentimes it is deep

down. The healing process is often delayed by insensitive

individuals who cannot tolerate the foibles of difficult people.

Tell them something like this: "I didn't like the way you made a

fool of me in front of those girls, just to appear cute. I hope you won't do that again."

The statement above is frank and yet open to give them a second

chance.

It gives leeway for improvement.

This is the proper way of dealing with difficult friends because it

also helps them to realize their faults and to change their attitudes.

Difficult Classmates

Classmates are not necessarily friends.

Most are acquaintances in your classroom. You share the same room, subjects, and professors.

Difficult students often want to prove something. In doing so, they need a tool to drive home a point. They seldom choose fellow difficult people for this.

Difficult classmates often choose the silent types who look

harmless and unpopular.

Popular people have support, and difficult people do not want a

mob to be against them. They can't stand majority rejection. In the

first place, they often try to prove something because they want admiration.

If you look like a harmless loner, you're likely to be chosen. So

beware!

he smart way of dealing with difficult classmates is to always

stay away from them. There can't be only two students in a

classroom - and there can't be only two chairs. Let others fill in the

need to be "tools" for them. The safest seat in class is near the teacher's table. Stay there. It is a refuge in a stormy classroom.

You are even safer outside the classroom. If your difficult

classmates eat in the canteen, eat somewhere else. If their team is up against your team in your sports class, stay out of their path.

Play those games where there is no physical contact involved from

your opponents, like volleyball.

If for some turn of events, you are teamed up with difficult

classmates for a project or some undertaking, plead your teacher for reconsideration. If the teacher proves to be another difficult person and refuses, then the best option is to yield.

Accept your difficult classmates. Try to enjoy their company; it

won't take forever. School projects last only for a time.

Laugh at yourself for the temporary misfortune.

Face it. There's no use worrying over difficult classmates who

have nothing better to do than project themselves as the main characters.

And you should know better; actually, they need help. Their egos

might be terribly hurt.

They are picking on you most probably because they see that you are a nice person. They regard you as a whole individual with a healthy character who can take on their impossible attitude.

So being picked on and still being nice about it brings out your

potential as a mature, rational individual.

Difficult Neighbors

Unless you plan to move out of the neighborhood, difficult

neighbors can affect not only you but your family and even your

pet as well.

The best attitude to have is to do what you want as long as it is

confined within your territory.

If they complain, politely point out that whatever it is you are doing that drives them crazy is being done on your property.

They may not let you alone even with the above polite explanation,

but at least you let them see that you know your rights and will stand up for them.

Now be sure that whatever you are doing within your property

directly affects only you and your family.

Don't watch TV, listen to the radio, or play your musical

instruments with full blast volume. Make sure the volume fills only the room where it should be heard.

Avoid having noisy parties into the wee hours of the night.

Make sure your howling dogs are confined to where your difficult neighbor won't hear them.

What if it's the other way around? What if your neighbors annoy

you until you can no longer tolerate it anymore?

You can give your neighbors a friendly visit and tell them your

woes. If they don't heed your appeal, take your case to the local authority. If this move doesn't work, then yield.

Just ignore the nuisance.

Most difficult neighbors need attention. Orient yourself and your

family not to pay attention to your neighbors' untoward behavior, but continue to be friendly with them.

In due time, they will grow weary of their actions and they will return the good favors you've been showing them.

Difficult Bosses

If bosses start being difficult, almost all your life can take a sudden negative twist.

Again, the best antidote is obedience.

Resigning is a temporary escape. If you transfer to another

company, you may end up with a worse scenario.

Console yourself with the thought that difficult bosses last only

some hours.

Relish at the thought of home.

Relish at the thought of warm food, peace and quiet, and then some

quality sleep.

The right thing to do is to stay positive as you remain being

obedient.

Life is more than dreading the company of your bosses. Learn to enjoy their company.

Your bosses may have needs they are not aware of, and you are

there to help them cope. It's a noble calling, really.

Finally, thoroughly enjoy your weekends by unwinding and doing

things you like.

You need the therapy that happy weekends bring to you relief from

the stress your difficult bosses put on you five days a week.

By doing this, you may then come out fresh and recharged for the coming week.

Difficult Business Partners

A business can be as valuable as life itself.

You have to watch out whom you partner with in business. Most

business partners are close friends, and starting a business with them is often a rewarding experience.

But money matters can pressure people and change them. The

business partners and close friends you thought you knew can slowly turn to difficult business associates.

This will terribly affect work relationships in the office, and the

business itself.

You may have common goals with your business partners, but your opinions may vary and conflict.

At times having standard work procedures may help stabilize

things; but at times they don't, especially if one of you starts to

play with the idea of bolting out of the partnership to start another business.

When business partners start being difficult, it is good to be open-

minded and flexible about things without compromising your principles and the company's agreed policies.

Often, differences in opinion do not necessarily mean a real

conflict is present. You must try to listen to the ideas of your

difficult partners and put in some of your own. This usually leads to a settlement.

Sometimes, the ideas of your partners may seem more effective

and lucrative, but it goes against the goal of your company. And in spite of your repeated pleas to preserve your mission-vision, they insist and threaten to part ways with their investment if you don't give in.

This is the time to review your partnership and be frank with each

other.

The company goal probably needs some adjustment or revision.

Why not agree together to consider modern trends and give the

company a new face?

But if things get out of hand, and if they want out, let them out; but make sure all ends in a positive, friendly note.

In any business relationship, especially one with difficult people,

assimilation is vital from both sides.

Both must give and take something.

If it is true in the investment aspect (both must share in the capital),

it should also be the same case in settling ideas.

Difficult Co-workers

Difficult workers are easier to handle because they are under company rules and regulations.

The best weapon against difficult co-workers is to be friendly to

them as you focus on your work.

When you have established yourself as a friendly co-worker to all,

you give lesser chance for difficult co-workers to recruit people to be on their side.

You are in a tighter situation if the difficult co-workers are close

friends of your bosses.

If you produce excellent and dedicated work for the company,

nobody can give you trouble. Your character and work attitude are

your best defenses in tight situations against difficult co-workers who have allies in high position.

In a worst scenario, if you are fired due to the machinations of

difficult coworkers, you may plead the attention of higher authorities.

Seek justice without compromising your character.

Don't hate anyone, not even the difficult coworkers and their

accomplices.

Show good attitude, even if the director himself fires you.

Persecuted good people will always end up with favor that is better

than what they originally had. You must have faith that this is the natural order of things.

Difficult Strangers

Strangers are the easiest to get rid of. But be careful on how you do it.

Make sure you act firmly but politely.

Use polite words such as "sorry" and "excuse me."

Never humiliate difficult strangers. If they start abusing you in

very scandalous ways, walk away from them and ignore the tirade of words they will send behind you.

Smile as you walk away.

Never look embarrassed or affected.

Chapter 9: How To Handle Difficult Topics

We have all experienced situations where we found it difficult to talk about an issue. It might be at home, in school or in the workplace. Sometimes we are unable to talk and let a situation go out of hand. Normally the difficulty in talking is brought by perception of encountering resistance from the people we are talking to. In the workplace, we experience situations where we were unable to offer feedback to another colleague or even to the boss. We are not sure how they will take it. We tolerate a performance problem unable to speak it out. All these situations will lead to perception that you are dealing with difficult people whereas it is us who avoided the difficult communication in the first place.

Positive communication is a skill we can learn that will enable us handle difficult topics as well as difficult people. We want to communicate in a manner that doesn't raise emotions. We should communicate in such a manner that those we interact with feel the need to maintain a positive interaction with us. In this way we avoid difficult situations. For instance, you want to talk to your child about substance abuse. You fear that they might get difficult and fail to talk to you about it. You need to dissociate your emotions and maintain a positive attitude to get as much from the discussion as possible. Positive communication doesn't mean we have to agree with the other party and what they say. Rather, we build an environment of trust and respect so that we are able to interact positively in the future.

When dealing with a difficult topic you need to:

Being brief

Be brief in your communication with a difficult person. This means you remain on the issue at hand without deviating to other issues not relating to it. Normally when we get angry, people tend to bring up old issues or frustrations into play. For instance we can start recalling when a colleague at work said something bad about us even though you had moved on from it. This only serves to escalate the situation. Keep it as short a possible but getting as much information as possible. Retain your focus throughout your communication. Being brief entails being very specific about what you are talking about. Address specific instances where you want action or explanations given.

Remain positive

Remain positive and choose to look at the wider picture. Even when you are dealing with a very negative person, do not be reduced to their antics such as name calling or accusations. Choose to be the bigger person. Making positive statements and requests makes a lot of difference. Practice marinating positivity in all your conversations. This doesn't mean you are nice and happy all the time, but when you are working with a difficult person, you don't need to escalate the situation by being difficult as well.

Offer to help out

This goes a long way in diluting a situation. You might be offering some minimal help but the fact you offered that help in the first place will make dealing with people a lot easier. Some people become difficult when they feel overwhelmed by work. If you are a boss, this would help them realize that you care for them and no matter the amount of help you offer, they'll feel more relived. If you are dealing with a friend going through a difficult period, offering them help enables them to open up to you and cease being difficult. Even with children, helping them out in small ways makes them feel loved. What bothers them might be a very small issue in your eyes.

Write it down

When you are anticipating to have a difficult talk with someone, it's important to play the conversation that may occur, then write it down. Focus more on your responses so that you can have a good grasp of the best way to respond. When you read through what you have written, you get to have better sense of how this may pan out. It will also enable you to decide when to lay more emphasis on certain words so that your communication hits home.

Respond decisively

When you deal with difficult people or situations, you need to act decisively. Never bring about doubt in regards to who you are and what you stand for. Be confident and speak with conviction. Work to avert a crisis by dealing with issues as soon as they arise.

People from all walks of life encounter difficult people and difficult situations all the time. It is how you deal with them and how you turn them around to your advantage that determines if you are really a great person. You should also look inside yourself to know if you are a difficult person as well. You might be the cause of the problems you are trying to solve in the first place.

Chapter 10: How To Deal With A Tactless Person

It can be very awkward and uncomfortable to be with a tactless person. Much more so when people around you recognize that the two of you are friends. Being friends with The Big Mouth should not be that discomforting if you know what to do and where she is coming from. Here are some tips on how to deal with such a person.

1. Don't take it personally

Being tactless is her problem, not yours. The important thing is still the way you treat others. Eventually, people will know that you are a different person and would not so much associate you with your friend if you constantly show them that you have your own personality. Be very careful, though, of being influenced by the attitude of your friend. Make sure that you stand firm on your principles and values and apply them accordingly.

2. Understand their situation

A lot of tactless people are behaving the way they do because of how they were raised as a child. Insensitive people are usually deficient of love, care, and attention from their parents or guardians when they were little, so they don't know how to go along well with others. Most of the time, they do not mean to be offensive, it is just that they honestly do not know how to say things appropriately. If you realize this, then you can develop a better understanding of where they are coming from.

3. Don't encourage their behavior

When you notice that someone is tactless, don't encourage by staying quiet every time she makes an insensitive remark. If you constantly affirm her opinions about other people or situations, her tactless behavior is fueled and she will think that it is okay. This is harder to do when you are talking to each other one-on-one, especially when she is criticizing another person and not you. Another way of calling this situation is gossiping. Never ever encourage gossip. What makes you think that she is not telling bad things about you, too? It is easier when she is being rude to you. Simply walk away and ignore the person. Doing so will convey a strong statement that you don't want anything to do with that kind of behavior.

4. Don't go into a dispute

Tactless people love confrontations. They actually thrive in them and it stimulates their sarcastic and know-it-all nature. Become aware when a conversation is heading to a state of disagreement and quickly change the topic or leave the room. It is impossible to win against a tactless person because: a.) she will use all the best condemnations against you, including all your personal flaws and physical defects if there are any, and b.) if you go down to her level and eventually manage to win the argument, you are still the loser because you just became a rude person yourself. The best thing to do is just smile and step away and let her defame herself, so to speak.

5. Forgive quickly

This is perhaps the best thing to remember when you encounter a tactless person. Whenever she says anything against you or critical of you, try your best not to retaliate and forgive her quickly, if not right there on the spot. You are actually the one that is at a disadvantage by harboring feelings of resentment for this kind of person. She may have long ago moved on from the incident, while you are still torturing yourself from her comments that are really not helpful in any way. When you immediately release forgiveness, you essentially take away her power to hurt you or upset you.

Chapter 11: Reflect Difficult Behavior Back

A risky but effective way to deal with difficult people is to give them a taste of their own medicine. Some difficult people do not realize how awful they are being toward you. Showing them their own behavior can help them realize that they need to make an attitude adjustment. Other people do not care if they cause you emotional harm or strife, but they will hate having their own behavior reflected back to them. They will probably leave you alone after tasting their own medicine.

You do not have to tolerate anything. When someone is being difficult, you may have the best luck trying to resolve the conflict using the tips in the previous two chapters. But you are certainly not required to always work with difficult people. You have the right to shut difficult people down when they try to add strife and hardship to your life. You may sometimes have the best luck being difficult right back to people. In addition, you may enjoy a cathartic release from putting someone through the same obstacles that he or she put you through.

Often, reflecting someone's difficult behavior right back to him or her will teach him or her a valuable lesson. No one likes to experience pain. When you hurt someone in the same way that he or she hurt you, he or she will not enjoy it. Some people will recognize that you did to them what they did to you, and they will grow regretful. They will adjust their behavior as an apology to you. You will teach them a very valuable lesson that they will probably never forget.

A great example of this is when you find that someone repeatedly manipulates and lies to you. Doing the same thing right back can be very helpful in teaching manipulators and liars how much their behavior hurts. Manipulate manipulative people. If you catch someone trying to manipulate you, you can put on a smile and reverse the behavior. For instance, if your romantic partner is being difficult and tries to pout to get you to leave a party that you wanted to go to, you can pull the same pouting act at an event that he or she makes you attend. If your spouse texts you and says that he or she will be working late, but you know that is a lie, you can say that you are working late as well and let him or her catch you in the same lie that he or she told.

When you are being manipulated, the genuinely best reaction is usually to do exactly opposite of what your manipulator wanted. Let's go back to our example of the manipulative partner who pouts to get out of social events. When you see this partner start to sulk and try to ruin the party for you so that you go home, do the opposite. Ignore your partner's childish behavior and start having a great time. Manipulators hate being thwarted and they will learn to try different antics if their usual ones stop working on you.

In customer service, it can be beneficial to lose all friendliness when dealing with rude customers. You can reflect unfriendliness back to people who are rude to you in any situation, but this method is especially great for customer service because it is discreet. While you should not be blatantly rude because of the conventions of polite society, especially in customer service, you can often show rude people how awful they are being by dropping your usual friendly demeanor and becoming stone cold instead.

Say someone walks into your department store and refuses to acknowledge your pleasant smile and cheery greeting. After looking around for a while, the customer decided to start berating you for not having the particular product that she is looking for. You do not have to maintain your extremely cheerful demeanor. You also do not have to be rude enough that you get fired. Strike a happy middle ground by losing your smile and becoming more unfriendly and professional. You are able to seem more respectable and you are able to reflect your displeasure to rude customers by doing this. I have had great success using this method in customer service. Some customers do not care if you are hurt by their rudeness, but most customers are just having bad days and will stop being rude when they see how much they have irritated or hurt you.

It can also be a blast to engage in verbal jousting with difficult people. This method is certainly useful in deterring mean co-workers or family, especially at events such as Thanksgiving. Your rude and querulous family members who have no boundaries and say whatever they want to you will be very surprised when you show up at next Thanksgiving full of equally insulting comebacks. People will be shocked that you have the audacity to speak to them the way that they speak to you. They will more than likely feel stung and back off from picking on you. In the future, they will fear your tongue and they will avoid making their usual ugly comments.

Fickle people are a waste of your time. They disrespect you by never giving you clear answers. You can reflect this behavior back on fickle people by not showing up. Be just as flaky back. Most fickle people will forget about you when you stop responding, and they will cease to be a burden on your precious time and resources. Others may realize how annoying and hurtful fickleness is, and they will change their ways.

You can definitely change a pessimist's tune by being extremely optimistic. Let your positivity outshine their rainy day parade. Refuse to let them drag you down.

A final great way to shut down deliberately difficult people is by remaining cool, calm, and unaffected by their behavior. Often, people try to get a reaction out of you. This reaction satisfies their cravings for attention or lets them know that they have succeeded in hurting your feelings. Do not take the bait and let difficult people provoke you. If someone is frequently able to draw you into a nasty argument, surprise him or her by suddenly just not responding to any provocations one day. There is often power in silence. You can definitely freak people out by refusing to give in to their petty jabs and attempts at hurting you. You will be the stronger person, and you will emerge on top in the power struggle.

It is entirely up to you if you want to get revenge on difficult people in your life. But if you do decide to be vindictive, do not feel guilty. You are getting cathartic release while teaching difficult people to respect you. However, keep in mind that these methods may backfire. Often, walking away or trying to reach an agreeable solution is the best option when dealing with difficult people.

Chapter 12: Don't Be Afraid To Set Consequences

In addition to the previous tip, it's important to remember that there are consequences for every action. You have to try to shift the balance of power to gain the respect of the bully. To do this, you shouldn't be afraid to stare the bully down.

Be articulate. Be reasonable. Be understanding. Don't be afraid to challenge the individual as well as to set ground rules or consequences.

One type of consequence that you can set is quitting your job or escalating things to a higher authority. This is a prime example of what you can or rather, must do whenever things get way out of hand in the office, such as when a manager or a team leader shows clear signs of harassing you.

It is also better if you ask for help from your co-workers, and especially those that have their own complaints to share about that one particular person as well.

Remember, as mentioned above, bullies hate confrontation, and will likely give in and leave you to do your job.

Then again, with the job economy as it is, threatening to quit your job isn't a luxury that everyone can afford. Besides, with the number of applicants out there, companies couldn't care less about you leaving your post because you can't deal with a certain person. If that is the case, you can take another measure, one that involves legal help.

For starters, it's easy to escalate harassment reports and problems to higher ups, and preferably to the HR department. If you know someone there, then better. If not, you should still file a report. It is more than likely that the aggressor will not want you to do this and will back off and leave you on your own instead. Besides, if the aggressor doesn't stop what they are doing, then it's only natural that you escalate things to have them taken care of.

If your company isn't keen on helping you deal with your problem, you can resort to hiring your own lawyer. Don't be afraid of the legal costs. This is because nothing is more expensive than your time and the amount of it that is wasted because of what the aggressor is doing to you. Also, if you're successful, you can ask both the company and the aggressor for a full reimbursement of the fees you're responsible for paying.

While all these things may seem like a hassle, if you let the bullying drag on for too long, it's not going to do you any good either. If an aggressor doesn't stop even if you threaten to escalate the problem, then it's only natural that you do it.

Remember, bullies aren't going to stop bullying unless you do something about it. Legal action is a perfectly good way to show the bully that you have the backbone to deal with their aggression.

Chapter 13: How To Deal With A Difficult Family Member

Most people have at least one family member who they deem to be difficult to get along with. They just seem to push your buttons, or perhaps you have a history with them that is hard to overcome. Finding a way to deal with this particular family member is critical to minimizing stress for you and others at family functions and other events.

Avoid Confrontation When Possible Many difficult people are either confrontational in nature or may easily turn even the slightest comment that you make into a major issue. Confrontations with family members are never pleasant. They can easily cause stress and tension with other family members too. Someone will have to make the decision to be the "bigger person" to avoid World War III erupting in your family, and this may fall onto your shoulders. It is important to understand what sets this person off and avoid giving them fodder for confrontation. While you certainly should not be expected to walk on eggshells around your family, some reservation around this person can go a long way toward keeping the peace.

When You Do Have a Confrontation

While your best efforts may help you to minimize the possibility of a confrontation, you may still find yourself involved in a heated argument with this person from time to time. It may be wise to remove yourself from the situation as soon as possible so that regrettable words muttered in the heat of the moment can be avoided. Once you have calmed down, consider making an effort to smooth things over. You may not want to apologize if you did nothing wrong. However, taking a few minutes to remind your family member that you love them and that you regret the argument may help you to get over this rough patch.

Establish Boundaries

One of the reasons that you may find your family member to be difficult to deal with may relate to boundaries. For example, the person may regularly say things that you find inappropriate or undermine your authority to your kids. This person may try to take advantage of you or otherwise cross different boundaries that you feel are reasonable. It is important that you clearly state what your boundaries are. Calmly but firmly point out the specific times when you believe your family member has crossed the lines that you have established. It may take them some time, but eventually, they may learn how to treat you how you want to be treated.

While these steps can help you to deal

more effectively with a difficult family member, there are times when the best medicine is space. Perhaps you will choose only to see them at family events, or only to speak with them on the phone occasionally. Reflect on the times and instances when this person has angered you and try to avoid those types of situations. This is a person who you may love but who you may not get along well with due to different personality types. Accepting that you may not get along with every member of your family is ok as well. Because of this, it may be best to establish some distance between the two of you.

Dealing with a difficult family member can be stressful and must be handled with sensitivity. As you incorporate these practices, remember that many do not want to abandon a family member, but healthy boundaries may also be necessary.

Chapter 14: Identifying And Managing Your Difficult Personality Traits In Conflict

We all have our own difficult personality traits that tend to flare up inside of us when faced with conflict. Achieving workplace goals and maintaining an emotional balance are possible when you recognize your personality strengths and limits. Difficult personality traits can be limiting and put you at a disadvantage when faced with conflict. You can work to recognize and manage these personal demons when it comes to confronting challenges.

Anger and Aggression
Aggressive behavior can detract from the point you are trying to make and may lead to dismissal. When you feel anger coming on, redirect your mind, or, if possible, walk away from the situation. Sigal Barsade, a University of Pennsylvania professor of management interviewed by The Wall

Street Journal, said it can be worth taking time off to avoid venting with coworkers, which can spread your negative thoughts like an "emotional contagion." It is better to take a sick day or vacation day to relax and calm down. This strategy can give you time to gain perspective on conflicts.

Passive-Aggressive Behavior

Lapsing into passive-aggressive actions may become another emotional contagion. Unfortunately, you may not recognize you are even acting in this manner. Psychiatrist Daniel K. Hall-Flavin, writing for the Mayo Clinic, describes this behavior as when your words do not match your actions. He explains that you may publicly agree to do something, even show enthusiasm for your agreement, and then sabotage the project in subtle ways. These tactics could include missing deadlines, complaining about your workload or becoming cynical or sullen. Therapy can help in these circumstances so that you can avoid this destructive behavior. If you find that your feelings often are out of balance with your work and resentment becomes a constant theme of your day, then you may need to look into other career opportunities.

Compulsive Behavior

Going beyond the call of duty may accomplish better work or help those around you meet deadlines. Some coworkers may see your extra effort as a threat or a tactic in trying to steal their jobs. Make the effort to respect job boundaries, which may help you avoid burnout. Dana Giota, a clinical psychologist, said in a 2009 Psychology Today article that it is important to be clear about your needs and expectations to others to maintain your own emotional balance.

Critical/Judgmental Behavior

Being the source of constant criticism and judgments of coworkers can lapse into career sabotage for yourself and others.

While you may think you are scoring points at the water cooler with unflattering information about coworkers, this can be a damaging source of gossip that could come across as bullying, according to a 2012 Forbes article. This type of difficult behavior is ripe for an exercise described by executive educator Marshall Goldsmith. His exercise starts with the sentence, "When I get better at …" and calls for you to finish the thought multiple ways to find the benefits of improving some aspect or behavior in your life. One person in Goldsmith's exercise found that saying, "When I become less judgmental," started him on a path toward discovering the benefits of letting go of judgmental thought patterns.

Try this exercise on your own to determine what difficult personality traits you may have. Then take some time to reflect on how you can handle yourself in a conflict situation and what you can do to improve.

Everyone can work on communicating better. When dealing with difficult people, you need to be careful that your weaknesses don't hinder you as you handle the situation.

Conclusion

Thank you again for downloading this book!

I hope this book was able to help you to learn how you can stay positive despite dealing with difficult personalities in the workplace.

The next step is to apply the lessons you have just learned in your own life.

Thank you and good luck!

www.ingramcontent.com/pod-product-compliance
Lightning Source LLC
Chambersburg PA
CBHW071451070526
44578CB00001B/306